I Love Sports

Basketball

by Allan Morey

Bullfrog Books

Bullfrog Books are published by Jump!
5357 Penn Avenue South
Minneapolis, MN 55419
www.jumplibrary.com

Library of Congress Cataloging-in-Publication Data

Morey, Allan.
  Basketball / by Allan Morey.
      pages cm. — (I love sports)
  Summary: "This photo-illustrated book for early
readers introduces the basics of basketball and
encourages kids to try it. Includes labeled diagram
of basketball court and photo glossary." — Provided
by publisher.
  Includes index.
  Audience: Age: 5.
  Audience: Grade: K to Grade 3.
  ISBN 978-1-62031-177-6 (hardcover) —
  ISBN 978-1-62496-264-6 (ebook)
  1. Basketball for children—Juvenile literature.
  I. Title.
  GV886.25.H64 2015
  796.323—dc23
                                              2014032108

Series Editor: Rebecca Glaser
Series Designer: Ellen Huber
Book Designer: Michelle Sonnek
Photo Researcher: Jenny Fretland VanVoorst

Photo Credits: All photos by Shutterstock except:
123RF, 6–7, 23mr; age fotostock, 5, 10–11; Alamy,
7, 16–17, 18, 23bl, 23br; Getty, 23br; iStock, 3, 14–15;
Thinkstock, cover, 4, 8–9, 23ml, 24.

Printed in the United States of America at
Corporate Graphics in North Mankato, Minnesota.

Ideas for Parents and Teachers

Bullfrog Books let children practice reading informational text at the earliest reading levels. Repetition, familiar words, and photo labels support early readers.

Before Reading

- Discuss the cover photo. What does it tell them?

- Look at the picture glossary together. Read and discuss the words.

Read the Book

- "Walk" through the book and look at the photos. Let the child ask questions. Point out the photo labels.

- Read the book to the child, or have him or her read independently.

After Reading

- Prompt the child to think more. Ask: Have you played basketball before? Have you watched a game? What did each player do?

Table of Contents

Let's Play Basketball!

Put on your sneakers.
Grab a ball.

Let's play!

Carlo has the ball.

He passes it.

Tim catches the ball.

Zach dribbles the ball.
He bounces it off the floor.

Ali shoots the ball.
She throws it up
at the basket.

The ball falls into the basket.

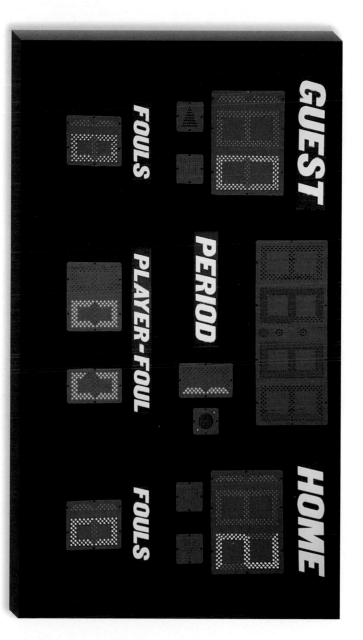

Two points!
Which team will score
the most?

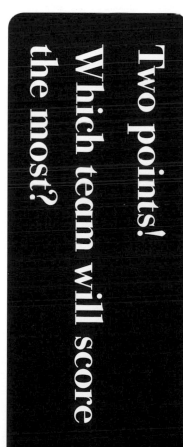

Now the other team gets the ball. They pass it toward the basket.

Mia puts her hands up.

She tries to block the shot.

But she bumps the other player.

Foul!

The player goes to the free throw line.

free throw line

18

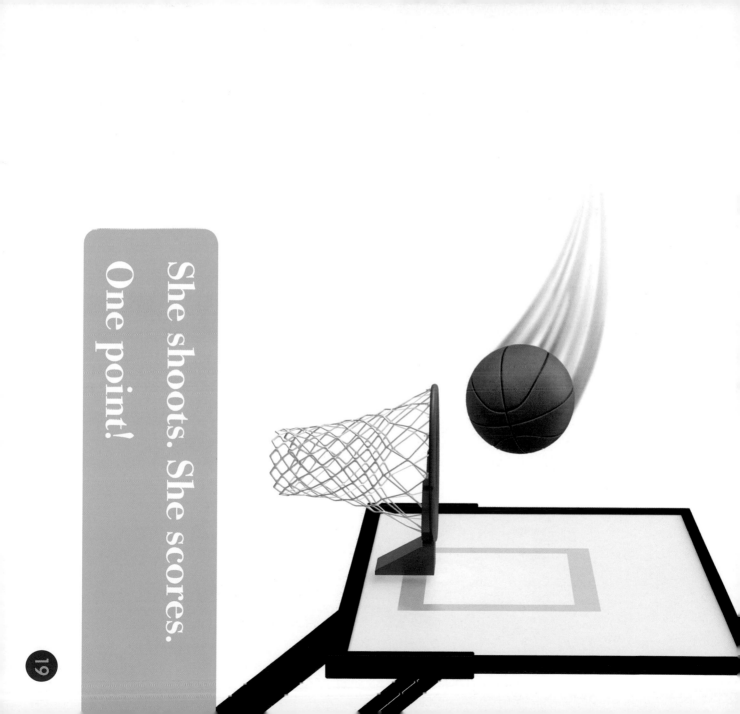

She shoots. She scores. One point!

Do you want to play? Take a shot. Swish! Basketball is fun!

On the Basketball Court

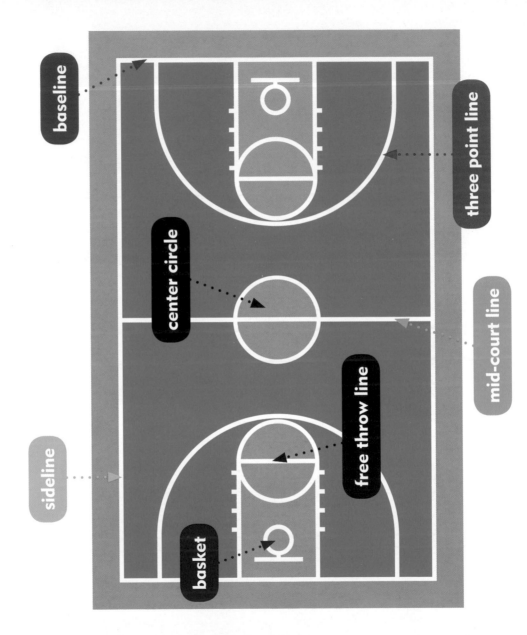

baseline

three point line

center circle

mid-court line

sideline

free throw line

basket

Picture Glossary

basket
What players try to get the ball through to score points.

dribble
To bounce the ball off the floor.

foul
When a player breaks a rule, such as bumping another player who has the ball.

free throw
A shot for one point with no one blocking.

pass
When one player throws the ball to another player.

team
A group of players who play together; there are 5 players on a basketball team.

Index

To Learn More

Learning more is as easy as 1, 2, 3.

1) Go to www.factsurfer.com

2) Enter "basketball" into the search box.

3) Click the "Surf" button to see a list of websites.

With factsurfer.com, finding more information is just a click away.